DATE DUE	RETURNED

MW01121472

HUMBER COLLEGE
LAKESHORE CAMPUS
LEARNING RESOURCE CENTRE
3199 LAKESHORE BLVD. WEST
TORONTO, ONTARIO M8V 1K

TITANICA

THE GREAT BATTLE GOWN,
EDMUND C. ASHER,
LONDON, 1968

TITANICA

THE GREAT BATTLE GOWN,
EDMUND C. ASHER,
LONDON, 1968

Sébastien Harrisson

Translated by
Crystal Beliveau

Playwrights Canada Press
Toronto • Canada

Titanica, La Robe des grands combats, Edmund C. Asher, Londres, 1968
© Copyright 2001 Sébastien Harrisson
Titanica, The Great Battle Gown, Edmund C. Asher, London, 1968
(translation) © Copyright 2007 Crystal Beliveau
First published in French as *Titanica, La Robe des grands combats, Edmund C. Asher, Londres, 1968* © 2001 Leméac Éditeur Inc., Montreal, Canada

Playwrights Canada Press
The Canadian Drama Publisher
215 Spadina Ave., Suite 230, Toronto, Ontario CANADA M5T 2C7
416.703.0013   fax 416.408.3402
orders@playwrightscanada.com • www.playwrightscanada.com

No part of this book, covered by the copyright herein, may be reproduced or used in any form or by any means—graphic, electronic or mechanical—without the prior written permission of the publisher, except for excerpts in a review, or by a license from Access Copyright, 1 Yonge St., Suite 800, Toronto, Ontario CANADA M5E 1E5 416.868.1620.

For professional or amateur production rights, please contact Playwrights Canada Press at the above address.

The publisher acknowledges the support of the Canadian taxpayers through the Government of Canada Book Publishing Industry Development Program, the Canada Council for the Arts, the Ontario Arts Council, and the Ontario Media Development Corporation.

Library and Archives Canada Cataloguing in Publication
Harrisson, Sébastien, 1975-
[Titanica. English]
Titanica : the great battle gown, Edmund C. Asher, London, 1968 / Sébastien Harrisson ; translated by Crystal Beliveau.

Translation of: Titanica : la robe des grands combats, Edmund C. Asher, Londres, 1968.
ISBN 978-0-88754-825-3

I. Beliveau, Crystal II. Title.

PS8565.A659T5713 2008   C842'.6   C2008-903212-8

This book was printed on 100% recycled stock.

Cover image: Jes Wojkowski; Cover design: Troy Cunningham
Production Editor: MZK

First edition: September 2008.
Printed and bound by AGMV Marquis at Quebec, Canada.

Titanica premiered in French on October 23, 2001 at the Théâtre d'Aujourd'hui in Montreal, with the following company:

TITANICA	James Hyndman
BLACK JACK	Yves Amyot
VIVIAN	Évelyne Rompré
ISADORA	Dominique Quesnel
JIMMY	Benoît McGinnis
EDWARD II	Stéphane Simard
QUEEN ISABELLA	Violette Chauveau
VIRGINIA I	Andrée Lachapelle
MAGGIE	Frédérique Collin
MR. CLARK	Gérard Poirier

Director:	René Richard Cyr
Assistant director:	Nicolas Rollin
Set designer:	Gabriel Tsampalieros
Costume designer:	Marie-Pierre Fleury
Lighting designer:	Martin Labrecque
Makeup artist:	Angelo Barsetti
Sound designers:	Georges-William Scott & Alain Dauphinais

The English translation of *Titanica* premiered on November 29, 2007 at Concordia University in Montreal, with the following company:

TITANICA	Joseph Bembridge
BLACK JACK	Adam Driscoll
VIVIAN	Natalie Mejer
ISADORA	Alexandra Draghici
JIMMY	Scott Humphrey
EDWARD II	Thomas Preece
QUEEN ISABELLA	Annie Murphy
VIRGINIA I	Joanne Poulin-Sarazen
MAGGIE	Emily Quaile
MR. CLARK	Ryan Hurl
SQUATTERS	Rio Mitchell & Michael Panich

Director:	Brendan Healy
Assistant director:	Erin Whitney
Set and props designer:	Dinah Weldon
Assistant set designer:	Sarah Tracy
Assistant props designer:	Jessica Hart
Costume designer:	Elisabetta Polito
Assistant costume designers:	Phillip Kadowaki & Katie Jean Wall
Lighting designer:	Ronan Kilkelly
Assistant lighting designer:	Zoë Gopnik-McManus
Sound designer:	David McLaughlin

Fight coach:	Jean-François Gagnon
Accent coach:	Nancy Helms
Assistant stage manager:	Michael Panich
Dramaturges:	Crystle Reid & Andrea Rideout

CHARACTERS

TITANICA	Fifty-year-old man dressed in a gown of steel
BLACK JACK	Ex-soldier
VIVIAN	Art history student
ISADORA	Scar face
JIMMY	Sixteen-year-old American stowaway
EDWARD I	Spectre of the King of England
QUEEN ISABELLA	Spectre of the She-Wolf of France
VIRGINIA I	Fictitious Queen of England
MAGGIE	Official Reader to the Queen of England
MR. CLARK	Spokesperson for Buckingham Palace
Band of squatters	
Soldiers	

SETTING

The action takes place in two areas of London: the King Edward II Dock (at the heart of which is a vandalized ship and several sealed containers) and the quarters of the Queen of England, at Buckingham Palace.

❧ PROLOGUE ❧

> Mr. CLARK, *alone on stage.*

Mr. CLARK   "London, the 16th of this month. England is delighted to announce that, after due consultation, the decision has been taken to develop the free zone, conceded earlier this year by Argentina, for ecological purposes. In fact, proud Albion…"

> THE QUEEN *of England appears mysteriously from the shadows.*

The QUEEN   Saintly. I prefer *saintly*.

Mr. CLARK   Saintly Albion, Your Majesty?

The QUEEN   Yes. The sound of the word alone casts a more flattering light on my reign.

Mr. CLARK   "Saintly Albion plans to create sumptuous English gardens there. To this end, the said zone, a seaside port, will be twinned with London's King Edward II Dock. This Friday, at an official ceremony marking the departure of the first ship bearing English flowers, Her Majesty Virginia I of England will inaugurate the restoration of the dock. In the coming months, more than a hundred floral species will set sail from King Edward to bloom on Argentinean soil. A symbol of fraternity, continuity and vitality, the English gardens in South America, envisioned and designed by some of our greatest landscape artists, will serve as a sanctuary, a true haven of beauty for the less fortunate of the world." It is in these words that your noble plans will be unveiled to the nation…

The QUEEN   I shall rid my country of an unspeakable evil…

Mr. CLARK   And garner the favour of militant ecologists, anti-monarchists and the press the world over. A remarkable feat!

> *MAGGIE enters.*

MAGGIE Your Majesty, if you don't want to miss the meteor shower announced by the astronomers, we'd best make for the balcony.

THE QUEEN Thank you, Maggie.

MR. CLARK There is one small detail: the squatters down on the docks have yet to be evicted. But by Friday, the authorities should—

THE QUEEN It is imperative. I will not let those miserable wretches sully this otherwise impeccable tableau.

MAGGIE Your Majesty, only six minutes before the start of the celestial ballet...

THE QUEEN I'm coming, Maggie.

MR. CLARK Your Majesty, regarding the emblem for the project...

THE QUEEN Oh, yes... what of this sculpture you proposed that we restore? This Great Battle Gown, Titania or...

MR. CLARK I reached the artist, the illustrious Asher...

THE QUEEN And?

MR. CLARK Well, he said it was up to the work of art to decide...

THE QUEEN I beg your pardon?

MR. CLARK It so happens that the work of art is itinerant; that it roams about the port and flees the instant one tries to approach...

MAGGIE A sculpture that scurries away and grants consent?

MR. CLARK This particular sculpture—this gown—is worn by a person.

THE QUEEN Well then remove the gown and put it on someone else!

MR. CLARK The person is an integral part of the piece. It's the very concept of the sculpture—

THE QUEEN Well, if the "concept" isn't willing to co-operate, the project will do without an emblem!

MR. CLARK This person is.... How shall I put it? Highly respected.

THE QUEEN It sounds as though you've made friends. You wouldn't be flirting with sculptures in your spare time, would you?

MR. CLARK No. I did, however, get wind of this person's good reputation.

THE QUEEN We'll do without an emblem.

MR. CLARK Yes, Your Majesty. As for the press release, I'll dispatch it to the media this morning.

THE QUEEN You are invaluable, dear Mr. Clark. As are you, Maggie. Not a day goes by without my thinking how fortunate I am to have two loyal allies with such an exemplary past. You are part of a great undertaking.

> *THE QUEEN and MAGGIE exit. MR. CLARK puts the press release into his pocket and looks out the window at the night sky.*

MR. CLARK Hell's Watchdog... reappearing to slash the sky of London on the eve of the announcement, after all these years. And what if we're making a terrible mistake?

∽ 1 ∾

> *The docks at dawn. TITANICA, a man dressed in a steel*
> *battle gown, stands at the foot of a vandalized ship. An*
> *enormous container is suspended from a crane. It rocks.*

TITANICA   Dawn breaks to reveal a ship in ruins. Look at it,
Titanica, do not tremble, do not fret, a mirror appears before
you to reflect your thoughts...

> *BLACK JACK's head appears from the opening in the*
> *ship. He shouts. TITANICA jumps. BLACK JACK*
> *bursts out laughing, leaps overboard and joins*
> *TITANICA.*

BLACK JACK   Even the old kings in their graves have stopped
pontificating; even the poets have given up verse to start
rapping. Sometimes I think: "She is so alone in her
reminiscing about the past that when she dies, all of History
will die with her." And do you know what, Titanica? It makes
me want to assassinate you.

TITANICA   You? Kill me, strangle me? Squeeze until my beautiful
blue veins are about to burst beneath my painted skin? Come
now!

BLACK JACK   You're right. I wouldn't dirty my hands. I was the
best shot in my regiment: I'd take you down with one bullet.

TITANICA   A fallen soldier combing the streets in search of a fight
in broad daylight, that's what you are. I'm untouchable, poor
Black Jack. Go sleep it off. You reek of alcohol and sweat.

BLACK JACK   I spent the night down at the docks with the
longshoremen. They asked me and two other blokes to
give them a hand. While I was at it, I thought I'd find out
what they knew about that government project. The old
warehouses are going to be razed to the ground next week.

TITANICA   They've been promising voters for years now that
they'd tear down those remnants of another era.

BLACK JACK   This time, they're serious. The Queen herself is
supposed to come down this Friday to inaugurate the work.

TITANICA   The Queen on the docks, against a backdrop of garbage cans and beggars! Black Jack, your sailor friends clearly had too much to drink. Don't you worry: those rusty old warehouses will long outlive us... *(Lifting her eyes to the sky, she notices the suspended container.)* Do they want to kill us? If that were to fall...

BLACK JACK   They stopped everything when they realized the ship had been struck. They'd barely started loading.

TITANICA   But they can't just leave this enormous container hanging over our heads! They'll start the crane up again, won't they?

BLACK JACK   When the ship's repaired. Not before.

TITANICA   A hole that big, in steel thought to be indestructible.... What could have possibly happened during the night that we should wake to such a spectacle? And all of these containers everywhere.... We're surrounded! What treasures could these enormous containers possibly be hiding?

BLACK JACK   They're filled with flowers.

TITANICA   They're too well sealed to be filled with just flowers. Perhaps they contain radioactive waste!

BLACK JACK   The ship was to leave London at the end of the week. Saintly Albion decided to create English gardens in Argentina! The dock will serve as the link between the two countries. And now we're going to be blamed for this act of vandalism. That's how they're going to wash their hands of us once and for all.

TITANICA   Every time they tried to evict us, we held our ground. We'll find a solution. We'll circulate a petition...

BLACK JACK   A petition! There are only ten of us left! We must take up arms.

TITANICA   You, Black Jack, are the only one in favour of arms. Isadora is vehemently opposed.

BLACK JACK   Isadora! Where is she now that the ultimate threat is at hand? Where is she when the tanks are at our doors and we stand huddled in the shadows of the warehouses waiting for the army to end our siege? Tell me, where is our leader?

TITANICA   Grieving the death of her brother.

BLACK JACK   If I hadn't brought her the London *Times* obituary page, she wouldn't even have known that DJ Lewis was dead. It's only a pretext.

TITANICA   Black Jack!

BLACK JACK   How do you explain the fact that we haven't heard from her for three days and three nights? She's been telling us to stay calm for months now, insisting that our claims will be met and that we won't be evicted. Sensing that all's lost, she must have jumped at the chance to flee.

TITANICA   You know nothing of diplomacy.

BLACK JACK   But I know weapons and from now on, they're our only chance of salvation. If they want war…

TITANICA   War! War again! When the paparazzi arrived this morning to film the ship, I wanted to implore them to stop fuelling public hostility towards us. But instead I hid between two warehouses and bit my tongue. I was afraid they'd recognize me and come after me in hot pursuit.

BLACK JACK   Those journalists would have mistaken you for an error of modern engineering.

TITANICA   An error of modern engineering! Not recognize me! In 1968, I was on the cover of every magazine, from *Time* to *Vogue*. Every single one! And now not only will my undying image go down in history but so too will my story, told in my voice and in my words. As you know, a young art historian is preparing a documentary on me…

BLACK JACK   You are a legend. The Great Battle Gown created by the extravagant Edmund C. Asher is a legend. Is that what you want to hear? You are a part of History.

We hear a woman's lyrical lament. TITANICA and BLACK JACK are taken aback. ISADORA enters, her face covered with a veil. She is carrying a bag.

ISADORA Now merely a shadow, I walk alone in this world. Your lost body, dear brother, confines me to darkness. And all too alone I go, dark, impenetrable and withdrawn, along the water's edge, where I can hear the incandescent song of the drowned.

TITANICA Isadora!

ISADORA On the morning of September 13th, I arose, firm in my resolve to go identify the body of DJ Lewis. I am his sister; the duty is mine. I put a black veil over my hideous face and went to the morgue. "Madam, I am his sister. Let me see him. Let me close his eyes so that he can begin his journey to the kingdom of the dead." An empty drawer, his name erased from the registry and the only trace of him, this bag, his personal effects, his only possessions, his whole life. "Let me see him! I am the last lucid member of his family on this earth; it is my duty to accompany him to the gates of the everlasting. Let me see him!" They directed me to the district cemetery. And so I walked, furious, ready to dig him up with my own nails if it meant I could finally close his eyes. His name on no stone, his body in no grave and the same stunned look from the guards. For three days and three nights, I visited all the cemeteries and all the morgues of London...

BLACK JACK tries to grab the bag that ISADORA is carrying.

No! This is all I have to remember him by, to get a sense of who he was...

BLACK JACK You never bothered visiting him while he was alive, and now you play the grieving sister? You wouldn't even recognize his face. He was a child when you saw him last!

ISADORA I'll know him when I see him. Once, I went in secret to an old warehouse where he was recording. I pressed my ear to the wall and listened to each of his tracks, one by one.

I may not recognize his face as a man, but I heard his heart, and for that I will know him when I see him.

TITANICA   We'll find him. Don't worry, we'll find him.

ISADORA   I have been without strength, without courage, without arms, without legs, ever since his body disappeared. Please, carry me to my quarters.

TITANICA takes ISADORA in her arms and exits.

୬ ‖ ୶

Once they've left the stage, BLACK JACK bursts out laughing.

BLACK JACK   Her quarters? Nothing but a couple of cardboard boxes filled with rotting rugs and mismatched cushions!

VIVIAN enters carrying a camera.

You're here to film the vandalized ship? Come on then, don't be scared.... You can even interview us, young miss.

VIVIAN   You're mistaken. I have a meeting with a lady. Titanica...

BLACK JACK   The pile of junk?

VIVIAN   The work of art.

BLACK JACK   You'll have to come back later.

VIVIAN   We're to meet in a quarter of an hour.

BLACK JACK   She won't be coming. A minor mishap.

VIVIAN   Nothing serious, I hope?

BLACK JACK   A breakout of rust.

VIVIAN   I'll wait. Our interviews mean a lot to her. She'll come.

BLACK JACK   So it's true, this documentary business that Titanica's been nattering on about for weeks. She calls you "my darling Vivian" and tells everyone that you're Asher's assistant.

VIVIAN   I'm not his assistant. I'm cataloguing his work, which is why I'm staying with him.

BLACK JACK   She also claims that you conduct your interviews with her in private, without breathing a word of it to your boss.

VIVIAN   Let's just say I don't bring up our interviews in Asher's presence.

BLACK JACK   Asher's quite well off, or so I hear. He gives Titanica a monthly allocation. You must do all right for yourself…

VIVIAN   That criminal getup wouldn't be a cover for a tax collector, would it? I think this conversation has lasted long enough. You'll tell Titanica I was here?

BLACK JACK   I shall, Miss Art Historian.

VIVIAN   That's very kind of you, sir. Goodbye.

BLACK JACK   Oy! We can drop the formalities. This is the docks, love, not the university!

◈ III ◈

The royal quarters. THE QUEEN and her reader. In the
distance, we hear the piercing howl of the dogs of the
royal kennel.

MAGGIE   *(reading)* "My Queen, my pussy, my beacon, my lady—I
say my lady and my beacon and my pussy and my Queen,
though I don't know how to spell them; yet, Virginia, my
mouth on your skin would trace the letters instinctively..."

THE QUEEN   From the beginning, Maggie.

MAGGIE   I really don't think it's—

THE QUEEN   And slower.

MAGGIE   *(with growing discomfort)* "My Queen, my pussy, my
beacon, my lady—I say my lady and my beacon and my
pussy and my Queen, though I don't know how to spell
them; yet, Virginia, my mouth..."

THE QUEEN   Who could this insolent character be? Go on...

MAGGIE   This is the seventh time this morning that you've asked
me to re-read these miserable lines, in an attempt to uncover
the identity of this anonymous poet. And yet your lover of
the docks and the underground, as he likes to sign his letters,
hasn't written for nearly two weeks.

THE QUEEN   Six months of a fiery correspondence and suddenly
nothing?

MAGGIE   No other letter bearing your name has been deposited
since this one.

THE QUEEN   Could the fountain of poetry be all dried up? What a
shame. I found it amusing.

MAGGIE   It seems to me there are more amusing pastimes than
receiving letters of a pornographic bent. Perhaps I could read
you a passage from that botany book you so admire?

THE QUEEN   And you looked closely in the spot where he usually
leaves the letters?

MAGGIE Yes, Your Majesty. Between the legs of Henry VIII I slipped my hand again and again. In vain. I went disguised this morning. Imagine if someone should discover that the Queen's reader goes to Westminster Abbey every morning to feel up the statue of Henry VIII in search of a missive left there by some hoodlum!

THE QUEEN This anonymous lover has a sense of humour I find quite delightful.

MAGGIE You're obviously not the one groping the anatomy of a statue every morning. This is perfectly ridiculous!

THE QUEEN I would say that it's perfectly picaresque.

> MR. CLARK *enters, his clothes in disarray.*

MR. CLARK Pardon my appearance, Your Majesty. It only hints at the perils I had to overcome to arrive at your door. Not a single pitfall was spared me en route from the docks to the palace —

THE QUEEN A pity your Queen has no desire to listen to you.

MR. CLARK Your Majesty, last night, the ship from your fleet moored at the King Edward Dock was... vandalized.

> *A beat.*

THE QUEEN The curse!

MR. CLARK I was about to deliver the press release this morning when the news reached my ears. I went straight to the scene and already the journalists were flocking...

THE QUEEN The predators!

MR. CLARK Everyone in London is talking. The people fear a new wave of terrorist attacks and the howling of your dogs, Your Majesty, which has been going on for days now, only adds to the widespread panic. What folly could possibly distract you from giving the order to feed the dogs?

THE QUEEN I knew the resistance of that handful of lepers would end up foiling my plans.

Mr. CLARK A source has informed me that the leader of the gang is in mourning. Her brother just died. Let's take advantage of their weakened state to reinforce security.

The QUEEN The curse!

∾ IV ∾

The docks. BLACK JACK takes a moment to himself.

BLACK JACK Homage to DJ Lewis. I owe a lot to DJ Lewis. As
much as a son to his father, a believer to his god. To DJ Lewis
and his music. His music which, when I first heard it, already
exposed the end coursing through his veins, as though his
death were flaunting itself on the dance floor, reminding us
that we, too, were in its grip. I was blown away by his tracks,
lost in the crowd of naive and innocent youth, when it hit me
that I wasn't one of them anymore, and that from then on, I
would walk alone towards another age I knew would bring
me closer to the grave where bodies go to rot. Watching them
smoke the same cigarettes, burn recklessly with the same
desires, go about, still full of illusions when I had already lost
mine… it was all so unbearable. For the first time, I realized
that life would go on after me. I REFUSE TO HAVE OTHERS
SEE A DAWN THAT I WON'T SEE. Suffocating, I left the
dance floor and took refuge in the shadows of an alley.
Breathe, breathe, cling to life, don't let it go, grab onto it, keep
it! Kneeling on the pavement, what was to become the
guiding line of my life appeared before me. A tiny word
written on the brick wall, a teenager's graffiti. Four letters:
K-I-L-L. If I have to die, I'll be the last. Everyone will perish
before me. After all life has ended, I'll go. I'll plant a huge
knife in the heart of the earth to keep it from turning, and I'll
go, relieved that no one will live after me. Thank you, DJ
Lewis. Rise up!

> *He walks around, banging on cans and calling as*
> *though he is ordering an assembly. Little by little, a*
> *group forms around him, made up of squatters who*
> *have appeared from the shadows.*

Until now, our refusal to engage in their bargaining tactics
has bought us time. But now our days are numbered. I see
only one solution: to take up arms. Who will fight by my side
to defend our rights? *(no answer)* It's our territory that's at
stake here! *(a beat, still no answer)* Fine. But don't come crying
to me when you're driven away at gunpoint!

જ V ન્

The docks. VIVIAN enters, frightened. Everyone gathers around her.

VIVIAN   I saw him, the guy who vandalized the ship, I saw him! Wandering around by the containers, pale as a ghost, I saw him!

A beat, then JIMMY enters, bewildered. He is carrying a knapsack.

TITANICA   *(touched)* A pale-faced little sailor! He looks freshly plucked from the painting of a Flemish master!

JIMMY   I'm not a sailor and I'm not Flemish. I'm from America.

TITANICA   Welcome to England, young American.

JIMMY   Thank you, ma'am.

TITANICA   Titanica. Call me Titanica. And your name is?

JIMMY   Jimmy.

BLACK JACK   This adolescent runt couldn't have struck the hull of a ship thirty metres high!

VIVIAN   He seemed taller in the shadows...

TITANICA   What brings you to our island, dear child?

JIMMY   Are you from the Young Conquerors Welcoming Committee?

BLACK JACK   The what?

JIMMY   The Young Conquerors. I crossed the Atlantic to join their ranks.

BLACK JACK   America is sending its scouts and missionaries! Run for your lives!

JIMMY   You're mistaken. It's a serious organization, with chapters all over the world. I have to go. By now, my host must be worried. I'm supposed to meet him on dock thirteen.

BLACK JACK   Oy! Wait a minute, kid. You think you can come into England, just like that? With a "Hi there, I'm Jimmy"?

TITANICA   This boy seems full of good intentions...

BLACK JACK   He's just an illegal alien trying to dupe British immigration.

> *BLACK JACK signals to the squatters, who grab JIMMY and are about to throw him in the water.*

JIMMY   Put me down! You'll regret it. Put me down!

TITANICA   Stop! *(The squatters stop what they're doing.)* Let's at least give the boy a chance to explain.

> *BLACK JACK grabs JIMMY's knapsack and rummages around in search of the young man's papers.*

BLACK JACK   If you cherish your life, you'll tell us everything you know about this organization right now. Rat them out or rot with the shipwrecks in the murky water.

JIMMY   Okay. But put me down first.

> *The squatters put JIMMY down.*

The Young Conquerors fight in the name of all, for greater justice and a more equitable distribution of wealth.

BLACK JACK   Oh, I get it!

JIMMY   No you don't get it; you think it's a joke. But you'll see. There are thousands of us travelling amidst the cargo in planes, boats and trains. Tomorrow, we'll upset the established power before anyone sees it coming.

BLACK JACK   And where did you hear about this organization? In the community bulletin?

JIMMY   On the Web. Once you've proven that you're a true activist and not one of those cops that hound them, they set up a meeting point. You bring your savings and a light bag and you're off for adventure. They only tell you your mission once you arrive to avoid any leaks.

BLACK JACK   Your mission?

JIMMY   Some are enrolled in environmental brigades, others are recruited by underground or anti-capitalist newspapers...

BLACK JACK   And how much of your nice American money did you give them?

JIMMY   They're not in it for the money. I only had two hundred dollars and they found me a place anyway.

BLACK JACK   Now that's what I call art! Feeding outdated ideals to the youth while emptying their pocketbooks!

JIMMY   I don't consider justice an outdated ideal.

BLACK JACK   Don't tell me you bought it?

JIMMY is silent.

TITANICA   If this young man was swindled, perhaps we should come to his aid.

BLACK JACK tears up JIMMY's passport and takes the bit of money in his wallet.

BLACK JACK   This young man has no papers and no money. Overboard!

The squatters grab JIMMY again.

JIMMY   Put me down! I'm sure that someone's waiting for me.

BLACK JACK   There is no dock thirteen. You have no business here.

JIMMY   You said if I told you—

BLACK JACK   The moral of this story is very simple: never trust a stranger, Jimmy Boy.

JIMMY   Put me down. I don't know how to swim!

TITANICA   This joke has lasted long enough.

ISADORA enters, veiled.

ISADORA   Put him down.

The squatters let JIMMY go.

Just because our backs are up against the wall doesn't mean we're going to start drowning innocent people.

TITANICA Isadora's right. This young man has had a long trip and needs to rest. Let's take his things to my place, Vivian.

TITANICA and VIVIAN leave with JIMMY. The squatters disperse. BLACK JACK and ISADORA remain, sizing each other up.

BLACK JACK The tide will take him back one of these days.

❧ VI ❧

At TITANICA's. TITANICA is singing the final notes
of a lullaby. Seeing that JIMMY has fallen asleep, she
leaves him and joins VIVIAN, who quickly shuts off her
video camera.

VIVIAN   You'll have to excuse me. But hearing you sing, capturing the magnificent resonance of your frail voice in your armour of steel is, I believe, a matter for posterity.

TITANICA   I dare say you are the only one in this country who cares if I'm remembered or not…

VIVIAN   That's not true. If you made a return to public life and consented to a restoration instead of being so stubborn, we would no doubt have the pleasure of seeing you on the cover of all the major magazines and on every television station.

TITANICA   Oh, this restoration business: a project among countless others, with its own docket number!

VIVIAN   The man from the government calls Mr. Asher's workshop almost every day. It must be serious for a gentleman to be so insistent.

TITANICA   And what does Edmund tell him?

VIVIAN   That the decision is yours.

TITANICA   He probably just wants to raise the stakes.

VIVIAN   Don't be so hard on him. I've seen him every day for six months now and he doesn't seem that uncompromising. I think he's sincere when he says that it's up to you. The ball is in your court.

TITANICA   When I left public life, I left it for good. Can I not finish my days in peace on these docks? I feel at home here, amidst these huge abandoned structures of steel. Only in my interviews with you do I relive what I once was.

VIVIAN   Tell me about it. Tell me what you carry inside, what you believe to be your personal contribution.

TITANICA   No. Not today, Miss Vivian. It would take too long, be too perilous. Fatigue… my failing memory… I'd have to start from the beginning. Repeat myself again.

VIVIAN   No, you never repeat yourself. Please.

VIVIAN turns the video camera on.

TITANICA   Edmund C. Asher…. He was thirty years old—ten years my senior—and already people were calling him the future of sculpture in England. It was 1967. Every evening, he'd come for his cup of black coffee to begin his day—night for everyone else—at the café where I was waiting tables. Yes, I was once young, was once twenty, was once a waiter! And I met an artist who told me I could be "different." The last customer of the night, Edmund C. Asher. I'd watch him drink his black coffee while I set tables for the next day and I'd say to myself: "Tonight this man is going off to redesign the world and you have nothing ahead of you but tables to set and clear and reset for the rest of your life." I was twenty years old and all I could see in my future was an endless string of restaurant tables, propped one on top of the other like a stairwell leading straight to my death. One night, I gathered my courage and approached him: "Mr. Asher, I, too, would like to redesign the world." He put his hand on mine and said: "Don't call me 'mister,' it's as though you want to keep me at arm's-length." That night, we went back to his studio in Chelsea. The first thing I saw when I walked in were these few sheets of steel which, at the time, stood lifeless in a corner. Edmund opened a bottle of wine and I started talking, talking as though my life depended on it. I told him how scared I was. Scared that my life had no meaning. Scared of dying before I really had a chance to give something back to the rest of the world. Scared of being nothing but an explosion of cells that comes and goes before ever having a chance to justify its existence. He told me that he understood, that he felt the same anxiety and that the only difference between him and me was that, one day, he had clung to matter, to bricks and iron and clay, and now, when the world spun too fast, he had an anchor. He talked about young people like us who went about frantic, unable to find our

place in the new world order, and how the old guard was
ready to crush us at any given moment. We were fragile and
his only desire was to build an armour for us. The Great
Battle Gown, as he called it. It was his way of helping us,
the most fragile, make our way through this century. Artists,
women, blacks, poets, dreamers, gays, Jews! Titanica: the
word was forever on his lips. Titanica! Titanica! As though
this word alone had come to symbolize his great dream.
What a visionary Edmund was! The winds of freedom were
blowing, and yet he was filled with dread. "Our freedom will
scare them. The self-righteous will strike back! We must be
prepared." That night, we became lovers. Every night after
that, I would go to his studio when the café closed. We would
make love, and then he would get out of bed to work, and I
would fall asleep, exhausted. The next day, I'd wake up to see
the sheets of steel, still in the same corner, slowly coming
together and taking shape. And then one morning, it
appeared as you see it today. Edmund hadn't slept a wink.
There he stood in the dawn light, staring at it while he
smoked a cigarette. I came closer and, in the look we shared,
it was clear we were thinking the same thing. It was as
though it had assembled itself on its own, while night after
night we'd made love in the studio. Who had made it?
Perhaps a god who had heated the metal. An architect god!
No matter. Edmund would sign it and I... I would wear it.
I would be its flesh. One day in January 1968, I stepped inside
and Edmund soldered the last joint of the bodice. I was
Titanica, the Great Battle Gown. He said to me: "There is one
thing that you alone must know. A line is engraved on the
inside of the skirt." He whispered it in my ear. Then he
added: "This line is what you have to pass on to humanity."
And the whirlwind began. I was invited to all the major
museums the world over. They couldn't shut me in, I was just
passing through. I walked amidst the stunned crowds with
Edmund at my side, proud as a peacock. A diva! The
symposiums, the *biennales*, the interviews.... All the big
reviewers swooned before me. Flashes sputtered, the front
page of *Vogue*, *Time*, *Life*! Until time, boredom, passing
trends.... When Edmund set up shop down by the docks

three years ago, I vowed never to cross paths with him. All right. That's enough. I've said it all.

VIVIAN   The line, Titanica. The one hidden under your skirt.

TITANICA   No. Not that. I won't tell you, Vivian. Not you, not anyone. Even if you have me repeat the story two hundred times, I won't ever utter it. It's part of what will live on after I die. If anyone thinks to look inside the gown before sending it to the smelting works. *(She gives her gown a light tap.)* That's where we're headed, old girl; people recycle nowadays!

✒ VII ✑

Queen ISABELLA enters, dressed in period attire. She approaches TITANICA and VIVIAN.

ISABELLA   Excuse me, I'm new to the neighbourhood and I…

TITANICA   Ms?

ISABELLA   The She-Wolf of France is what they call me.

TITANICA   The She-Wolf of France! What an elegant and stylish title!

VIVIAN   It's from a Thomas Gray poem, I remember:
"She-wolf of France, with unrelenting fangs.
That tear'st the bowels of thy mangled mate."

TITANICA   So, Madam has inspired poetry. I, too, was the muse of a contemporary artist.

ISABELLA   I would like to know, sir…

TITANICA   Madam. One says madam to an artist's muse. Let me introduce myself: *TITANICA, the Great Battle Gown, Edmund C. Asher, London, 1968.*

ISABELLA   I was wondering if you've seen my husband, by any chance. I've been looking for him for an eternity. Seven centuries, to be exact.

TITANICA   *(to VIVIAN)* She must be an actress. From Stratford, no doubt.

ISABELLA   A tall man with red hair, dressed in clothes befitting another era, who speaks in parables and runs like a hound. His name is Edward.

TITANICA   I don't know anyone who fits that description. Do you, Vivian?

VIVIAN   No, I don't.

ISABELLA   Are you sure? You see, my husband is dangerous. Consumed by the fires of hell, he delights in inflaming the hearts of the pure…

TITANICA (to VIVIAN) Delivered like a true actress.

ISABELLA He does strange things sometimes.

TITANICA Such as?

ISABELLA Well, he has a soft spot for pretty young boys.

TITANICA For a married man, that is a touch bothersome.

ISABELLA A touch. And... he bites.

TITANICA That is a very bad habit. But alas, we haven't seen him.

ISABELLA In that case, can you tell me where I might have the best view of the surroundings?

TITANICA The old Atwood factories tower. It's a bit tricky getting up there, but the view can't be beat. We would be happy to accompany you.

ISABELLA How very kind. From there, I may be able to spot my husband.

TITANICA Take my arm, Madam She-Wolf of France. And you, Vivian, shall light the way. While our little angel is resting, let's be of service to this poor, devastated woman.

All three exit, leaving VIVIAN's equipment behind.

∽ VIII ∾

EDWARD enters on the run. Seeing JIMMY, he approaches with the utmost discretion, fascinated.

EDWARD   Such a resemblance... could it be? *(moving closer)* The same profile, the same delicate features...

EDWARD is about to touch JIMMY but just before he does, JIMMY awakes with a start. EDWARD hides quickly.

The same fiery look...

JIMMY checks his pockets and his knapsack. Seeing that everything has been stolen, he looks around for something to steal in turn. He grabs VIVIAN's video camera and goes through TITANICA's things in search of money, and is about to take off.

Young man!

JIMMY quickly slips VIVIAN's video camera into his knapsack.

JIMMY   What do you want?

EDWARD   You, young friend, bear an uncanny resemblance to a man who lived a long time ago: Piers Gaveston.

JIMMY   I don't think we're related. Who are you?

EDWARD   A hunted man who occasionally stops his flight to admire a pretty face.

JIMMY   Sir, you wouldn't be the special envoy from the Young Conquerors?

EDWARD   From where?

JIMMY   Never mind. I came here in search of a mission, but I think I'm better off looking somewhere else.

EDWARD   A mission on your frail shoulders, dear boy?

JIMMY   I'm not scared of anything and I know how to fight.

EDWARD   Well, then I have the just thing… I—as you see me, wandering the docks with my head hung low to keep from being noticed—am planning to fulfill a need for vengeance several centuries old, to avenge the memory of the man who was dearest to me and whom a queen had deported out of pure hatred. I'm the one who struck that ship last night…

JIMMY   Those freaks took me for the culprit and almost threw me in the ocean.

EDWARD   Can you keep a secret? I bite.

JIMMY   You bite?

EDWARD   Burning with a secular rage, I've come back to settle the score with this country. Soon, London will see a true revolution break out!

JIMMY   A revolution? Here, on the docks?

EDWARD   Yes. But for my plan to work, the squatters must stand up to the monarchy as long as possible, and take up arms if need be. Will you be my ally and try to convince them?

JIMMY   What will I get out of it?

EDWARD   You'll be on the front lines, just as you'd hoped!

JIMMY   That's what the Young Conquerors said and look where that got me!

EDWARD   In just a few days, these docks will be the scene of a great revolution!

JIMMY   Judging from their welcome, I'm not so sure they'll listen to me.

EDWARD   You'll find a way, precious child. And give them this enigma to ponder: "What flowers would fair England rather see grow in fields far from her own?"

JIMMY   What do I do if I want to see you again?

EDWARD   Just call me. Come here, to the water's edge, and shout. My name's Eddy.

JIMMY   I'm Jimmy.

EDWARD   And don't worry about the video camera. It'll be our little secret.

꙳ IX ꙳

The royal quarters. THE QUEEN, *alone. A forest of
miniature rosebushes has taken over the room.*

THE QUEEN The curse! From Edward II, the sodomite, who
humiliated his wife, Isabella of France, to Edward III, their
son; from Richard II to Henry IV; from Henry V to Henry VI
to Richard III who had his brother's children killed and
whose reign was one of terror; from Henry VII, the first of the
Tudors, to Henry VIII who created the schism and had his
wives decapitated; from Edward VI to Mary Tudor, Bloody
Mary, persecutor of the Protestants, to brave Elizabeth I, who
brought order and integrity to England; from James I to
Charles I; from Charles II to James II; from William III to
Anne Stuart, who reunited Scotland and England to
consolidate the kingdom; from George I to George II; from
George III to George IV; from William IV to Victoria, Queen
of England and first imperialist of India; from Edward VII to
George V to Edward VIII who abdicated the throne to wed a
divorcee; and from George VI to me, Virginia I of England:
can it be that a drop of blood has made its way through seven
centuries of history, from vein to vein, family to family,
marriage to marriage, war to war, regime to regime; that one
drop, one lone drop, has entered my blood to make me, in
turn, the Cursèd Queen of England? My father forever
insisted that, from century to century, the mad gene of
Edward II could only have died out. And yet, here I am, alone
in the eye of a storm where wind and tide converge on me.
Be strong! Think of Isabella, the She-Wolf of France, the
unfortunate wife of that Cursèd King, who held her head
high despite everything and had her husband's favourite
deported. And you, Edward II, whose reign was one of chaos,
you who wanted to change the order dictated from heaven to
earth, who put a man in your bed and folly at the head of the
nation: know, Edward, that I will not let you drag our island
down in the murky depths to which you have sunk. I will
purify England in the face of all adversity! As of today, I will
resume my study of botany.

MR. CLARK *enters, with* MAGGIE *close behind.*

TITANICA / 33

Mr. CLARK   Your Majesty, the hall and the master stairwells are overrun with miniature rosebushes! Everyone in the palace has scratched knees!

The QUEEN   I know. I'm receiving a journalist from the BBC this afternoon and our press secretary thought it appropriate to convey my passion for botany. Anything else?

Mr. CLARK   The House of Lords was wondering if we shouldn't postpone the ceremony, given the state of the ship.

The QUEEN   That is out of the question. The journalists will simply have to photograph the side of the ship that's intact!

Mr. CLARK   There is also the squatter issue. They're mobilizing.

The QUEEN   Incompetent good-for-nothings!

Mr. CLARK   The authorities did all they could. We can't very well ask the army to—

The QUEEN   Is there not a more peaceful way to keep those wretches on a leash?

Mr. CLARK   There is one. One alone that could get them on our side, that could nip their yapping in the bud...

The QUEEN   Do tell.

Mr. CLARK   We make Titanica our emblem. That man is one of them, he will know how to talk to them...

The QUEEN   A man?

Mr. CLARK   Actually, the artist's ex-lover...

The QUEEN   A man in a gown of steel?

Mr. CLARK   A man in his fifties, a gentleman. Everyone in London is aware of Asher's sexual preferences.

The QUEEN   A fruit as the emblem of my country?

Mr. CLARK   A homosexual, Your Majesty.

The QUEEN   A fruit, a homosexual, a dubious, aging man who insists upon affecting a young girl's giggle! I can just imagine. An object of disgrace whom, to top it off, is one of them!

Mr. CLARK   Then we'll need the army.

The QUEEN   Fine. Let the army invade the docks! With all your years of diplomatic experience, it is inconceivable that you could envision such an extravagant alternative. A fruit!

Mr. CLARK   The Lords were also wondering if Her Majesty, in spite of the recent terrorist acts, still plans on attending the ceremony in person.

The QUEEN   This Friday, Her Majesty will stand tall on the King Edward II Dock, terrorists or no terrorists.

>   *MR. CLARK exits.*

Maggie, perhaps you could read me one of my lover's poems, to get our minds off things?

MAGGIE   With the army invading the docks, at least one thing's for sure: you shan't be hearing from him again.

The QUEEN   No?

MAGGIE   He's a poet, Your Majesty. They'll make mincemeat of him.

The QUEEN   It would be sad for a titillating story like ours to meet such a cruel end.

MAGGIE   Your soldiers' zeal will silence that good-for-nothing once and for all.

The QUEEN   Hurry, Maggie, run, catch Mr. Clark! We *will* have that outdated fruitcake restored!

MAGGIE   Your Majesty…

The QUEEN   I will not have on my hands the blood of a poet who sang my glory.

>   *MAGGIE exits.*

꙾ X ꙺ

*Dawn. BLACK JACK has returned from the city, a
newspaper in hand. He bangs on things to rouse the
others. TITANICA, JIMMY and a few squatters appear.*

BLACK JACK *(reading)* "London, this morning. A rumour has
been circulating to the effect that the army will be sent in to
crush the siege of the King Edward squatters. Though the
royal palace was quick to deny these claims, a source that
wishes to remain anonymous confirmed that the army is in
fact on standby. Will we see the army invade the docks in the
next few hours?" They're making good on their threats.

TITANICA Calm down, Black Jack.

BLACK JACK It'll take more than the army to get rid of me, that's
for sure. They'll see what we're made of.

TITANICA Our young traveller heard a voice in his sleep that
made him privy to quite the enigma…

JIMMY No, it was a man, a man on the run. He was dressed in
extravagant clothing and claimed that a great revolution
would soon break out.

BLACK JACK Another drunk who takes his delusions for reality.
So what is this enigma, Jimmy?

JIMMY The stranger said: "What flowers would fair England
rather see grow in fields far from her own?"

BLACK JACK It could be irises, gladiolas, orchids or thistles for all
I care. Our lives are at stake here! *(brandishing the newspaper)*
This is a declaration of war, not a botanical treatise.

JIMMY He also said that we must continue to stand up to the
monarchy. Even if it means taking up arms.

BLACK JACK Now you're talking like a man, kid. But to take up
arms, we have to convince Isadora and her followers.

TITANICA All is not lost. Let's see what the child can do. Jimmy,
could you not try to convince Isadora?

BLACK JACK   This kid, change Isadora's mind? What a joke!

JIMMY   If she wanted to see me spared, maybe she'll listen to me.

BLACK JACK   I'll tell you what, Jimmy Boy: if you convince Isadora to let us take up arms, you'll become my right-hand man. But if you fail, I swear in front of all present that the tide will take you back.

JIMMY   Deal.

> *A beat.*

BLACK JACK   What?

JIMMY   It's a deal, Black Jack.

ஒ XI ஐ

*VIVIAN, alone. Queen ISABELLA enters dressed as a
museum curator. She is carrying an attaché case. She
fakes a very pronounced Italian accent.*

ISABELLA   *Scusi,* Miss. If I'm not mistaken, you are the assistant of
Mr. Asher, the great sculptor…

VIVIAN   Yes. Actually, I'm cataloguing his work.

ISABELLA   Let me introduce myself: Carlotta Spontini, curator of
the Contemporary Art Museum of Roma. I would like to have
a word with Mr. Asher.

VIVIAN   I'm sorry, but he doesn't see visitors. If it's about royalties
for exhibitions—

ISABELLA   It's about a commission, actually.

VIVIAN   Mr. Asher hasn't produced work for an exhibition in over
twenty years, Madam.

ISABELLA   Let me make myself clear. I'm not talking about pocket
change, but about money, lots of money… *(She opens her
attaché case in front of a stunned VIVIAN.)* May I? Our museum
is organizing an exhibition on intolerance. We are collecting
pieces by various European artists such as Wolfgang Klaus,
the famed Auschwitz painter, and Clara Miranis, the highly
esteemed war photographer. But we are missing an opening
piece for the exhibition, a pièce de résistance, if you will. I
would like to commission something from Asher: a metallic
muzzle of human dimensions. What more eloquent
illustration of human intolerance than a muzzle?

VIVIAN   He doesn't sculpt anymore.

ISABELLA   Surely there are a few scraps lying around his
workshop.… A bit of solder, and the deed is done.

VIVIAN   Mr. Asher is an artist, Madam, not a mechanic.

ISABELLA   One hundred and fifty thousand pounds. It's not
nothing. In the contemporary art world, people talk. Mr.

Asher's fortune is going up in smoke, creditors' notices are piling up on his doorstep...

VIVIAN   That is Mr. Asher's business.

ISABELLA   If I'm not mistaken, Mr. Asher has.... How do you say? A dependent... a beneficiary...

VIVIAN   Yes, a... an old friend.

ISABELLA   An "old friend" can be quite a burden. It would be a shame for this person to find himself living in even greater misery. One hundred and fifty thousand pounds! Perhaps Mr. Asher would make an exception.

VIVIAN   I could talk to him.

ISABELLA   What a charming young lady. Oh yes, there is one thing. I am flying to Roma tomorrow and would like to bring the piece back with me.

VIVIAN   Well, that's out of the question!

ISABELLA   (*closing the attaché case*) A pity for the old friend on misery's doorstep.

VIVIAN   Wait... in steel or in bronze?

ISABELLA   Whatever's more resistant. That's what counts. *Arrivederci*, Miss.

> *VIVIAN exits.*

(*dropping the accent*) I adore the flexibility of artists.

❧ XII ☙

Near ISADORA's quarters. JIMMY is about to enter but ISADORA comes out to meet him.

ISADORA   They sent you to urge me from my retreat. To coax the grieving sister out of darkness, much like they use electrical charges to jolt a crazy man from the depths of his delusions. And they plan to take up arms, do they not?

JIMMY   Who told you?

ISADORA   Nothing escapes me. The din of the docks always finds its way here.

> *ISADORA extends her hand to be kissed. JIMMY does so, awkwardly.*

When you have the stuff of a real revolutionary, you'll drop the formalities, and you will not kiss, but bite.

JIMMY   Black Jack said you'd be hard to convince. You no longer seem to be in mourning. Still veiled, but…

> *ISADORA lifts her veil, revealing her disfigured face. JIMMY is taken aback.*

ISADORA   My face frightens you?

JIMMY   No, of course not.

ISADORA   They didn't warn you? It's a gruesome tale. On the way to school, a stray dog appeared out of nowhere, knocked me down and bit me in the face. The pretty little girl, suddenly scarred beyond recognition. When the surgeon told my mother that the marks were permanent, she flew into a rage. She started screaming that she would kill the mongrel dog that had ruined the future of her precious daughter. She who had dreamed of marrying me off to a prince ever since I was born.… She threw my things in the street and told me that was the place for mangy dogs. I left, my dignity intact, but my heart heavy at the thought of being separated from my younger brother.

JIMMY   The brother you're grieving?

ISADORA   Lewis. He was the one she tormented after that. She wanted him to become prime minister. He disobeyed and became a DJ. DJ Lewis. For months, my mother followed him to the warehouse and implored him to set his sights higher. She would stand in the middle of the dance floor and hurl insults at him. Every time, security had to intervene. Then one night, at the end of his rope, he cracked: "I'm going to die, Mum. I'm going to die! It's already coursing through my veins. Hundreds are dying of it every day and nobody has a cure for this monstrous sickness. I'm going to die, Mum!" After that, my mother abandoned him. She left him to die alone. Widowed, disappointed and deserted, she got a job with the Crown. The end of her absurd dreams of power: serving where she would have liked to see us reign.

JIMMY   You've got every right to be devastated by your brother's death.

ISADORA   If only I could have closed his eyes, the eyes of my music-loving little brother. I put on a veil so that his last vision on earth would not be that of my hideous face. But his body had disappeared.

JIMMY   I hope with all my heart that you find him.

ISADORA   What did Black Jack promise you if I agreed to let you take up arms?

JIMMY   That I'd become his right-hand man.

ISADORA   You will be his heart. That's what's keeping Black Jack from becoming a great leader: a heart that can be moved.

JIMMY   Thank you, ma'am.

ISADORA   I tried everything to keep us from being evicted. I sat in the aisles of public libraries, poring over law books in search of legal arguments. I thought that justice was a clear and luminous book that opened the gates of truth to all. I was so determined. Until grief melted the heart of the warrior. Is there not a peaceful way to remind the powerful that our lives are worth as much as theirs? I would like to think so, but with Lewis to find, I haven't the strength to entertain such utopian ideals. Go now!

JIMMY   Thank you, ma'am.

> *ISADORA offers her hand to be kissed.*

ISADORA   Bite!

> *JIMMY hesitates then bites. He exits.*

ᔔ XIII ᔒ

VIVIAN is watching video excerpts of her interviews with TITANICA.

VOICE OF TITANICA   "I've filled out a bit with age. The space between the gown and me has almost disappeared. It's become quite cramped. That has to be the worst of it: the cold of the iron on my skin, the weight against my ribs, and the creak of the joints when I sigh." *(VIVIAN fast-forwards.)* "Edmund was in an awkward position. The man he loved was also his work of art. And because an artist often develops a kind of aversion towards his past work, he ended up neglecting me and our relationship fell apart." *(VIVIAN fast-forwards again.)* "Take it off, cast it aside? Oh, my dear child! Don't you think I've considered that? But what would I be without it?"

BLACK JACK enters.

BLACK JACK   Still probing Titanica's secrets...

VIVIAN stops the video.

VIVIAN   And you? Still looking for young idealists to engage in bare-fisted battle against the riot squad?

BLACK JACK   Our uprising will put a spanner in the works.

VIVIAN   If your uprising ever sees the light of day, it will probably end in a cloud of tear gas. *(a beat)* By the way, Black Jack, if it was your brilliant idea to steal my video camera, I want you to know that it won't jeopardize my project in the least. I've already started editing and I have enough material for three documentaries.

BLACK JACK   I didn't touch your camera. But if I were you, I'd keep an eye on that footage. Accidents happen all the time...

VIVIAN   Don't even think about tampering with my material. This documentary is extremely important for Titanica.

BLACK JACK   And you honestly think that's how you're going to change the world? By filming Titanica's ramblings and cataloguing the work of that senile old Edmund C. Asher?

VIVIAN   How dare you speak of them in those terms! When I first started doing research on them in university, everyone tried to convince me that Titanica was old news. But I didn't listen. Now the government is planning to have her restored and my work is met with interest.

BLACK JACK   But what does that give you? What do you want, Vivian?

VIVIAN   I want to recover a voice that's been lost. I spent a long time looking for my true calling. I tried my hand at everything: sculpture, painting, writing, cinema. Only to come to the conclusion that I'm not an artist. But if I can make the voice of those who have that talent heard, I'll feel as though I've accomplished something.

BLACK JACK   Humble servant of Art! Voices are being lost by the millions in this country, and you worry about reviving a cry that dates back thirty years!

VIVIAN   What about you, Black Jack? What do you want? To be the one responsible for their last cry? I am calling my documentary "The Archives of Humanity" and it will be my personal contribution, as small as that may seem to you.

BLACK JACK   "The Agony of a Pile of Scrap Metal" might be more catchy.

VIVIAN   Poor Black Jack. I know it's ambitious and that our bodies are headed for rot and oblivion. And maybe even our souls die. But that's just it! We have children to preserve the race, so why not ensure that our souls live on by conserving the manifestation of their essence? Every time I immortalize the thought of an artist, I feel as though I'm taking part in the Archives of Humanity, as though I'm keeping a soul from dying with the body that housed it.

BLACK JACK   I don't need the souls of those who've gone before me. I've got enough with my own.

JIMMY enters.

Did our American warrior accomplish his mission?

JIMMY Isadora has accepted that we take up arms.

✎ XIV ✎

TITANICA enters, a letter in hand.

TITANICA Dearest Vivian, I have the most incredible news, something that could have significant consequences for the future of our little community. Everyone, gather around!

A group forms around TITANICA.

For several years, I had a suitor.

VIVIAN I wasn't aware of any romance!

TITANICA To be honest, I'd almost forgotten myself. But today the gentleman resurfaced.

BLACK JACK The past again!

VIVIAN Black Jack!

TITANICA The British Embassy in Paris. The last stop on our journey. We had toured all the major museums on the planet and now the highest diplomatic spheres awaited us. Our crowning glory! The world leaders were inviting Art to their table! Such contempt. That night, in that marble, garishly lit room, I was the unhappiest work of art of all time, because I was alive. Oh, if all the paintings, all the sculptures, all the books could howl their chagrin! If they could put into words the despair that grips them when the so-called big wigs of the world look upon them. That night, my friends, I lived the drama of art. My soul in pieces, I was about to leave the embassy by the emergency exit to throw myself into the waters of the Seine when someone called my name. Oh! He had a certain *je ne sais quoi* that couldn't help but bring a smile to your face. "Let me introduce myself: William Clark, political attaché. Could we see each other again before you leave for London?" he asked, while adjusting his bow tie. The next few days, this Clark fellow kept sending flowers to my hotel. It infuriated Edmund. My schedule didn't allow for a second meeting. Of course it was flattering, but at the time I was still crazy about Edmund.

BLACK JACK And how, may I ask, does this story concern us?

VIVIAN   Black Jack!

TITANICA   Patience, I'm getting there. This morning, I received an official letter announcing that I have been chosen as the emblem of the England-Argentina project. My presence at the inauguration this Friday would be most appreciated and the invitation states that all of my friends—that would be all of you—are welcome to attend.

VIVIAN   So we won't be evicted!

TITANICA   For the occasion, I will appear beside our dear Queen, and a celebrated photographer will take pictures that will be sent off to all the major magazines. Believe it or not, the letter is signed by Her Majesty's official spokesperson, Mr. William Clark.

VIVIAN   You fraternized with the spokesperson of Buckingham Palace in your youth?

TITANICA   Yes, indeed! And it seems that he is the one behind my restoration project. I had no idea what had become of him. I had almost forgotten him. But he obviously remembers me. It's true, I had renounced public life, but...

BLACK JACK   Oh! The pain of clinking glasses with dignitaries. Such courage, such a sacrifice!

TITANICA   Be as sarcastic as you like, Black Jack. But the fact remains that our lives will be spared because of me, because of this suffocating skin of steel, and not because of weapons. You all know very well that it is against my principles to use my contacts in this way. But today's events demand it. I will speak personally with the Queen. I already know what I'll say.

BLACK JACK   This is absurd. The only solution now is to take up arms.

TITANICA   Things will be settled with class, between women of the world.

BLACK JACK   Even Isadora came to her senses. Come on, Jimmy. We must act.

BLACK JACK and JIMMY exit.

TITANICA   Poor Black Jack. You have to keep up with the times. It's no longer on battlefields that the real battles are fought.

VIVIAN   I am so happy. You, as the emblem of a national project! That's a huge honour. May I accompany you?

TITANICA   Of course. You will be my lady in waiting. Perhaps better days are on the horizon, dear Vivian.

❦ XV ❧

The royal quarters. THE QUEEN and her reader.

THE QUEEN   Tomorrow, Virginia, I shall rid her country of an unspeakable evil.... Tell me, Maggie, are there no new chapters in this mysterious correspondence?

MAGGIE   Thankfully, no. Not a single pornographic note.

THE QUEEN   Now, now. No need to be so harsh. Who knows, perhaps tomorrow on the docks this intriguing character will seize the opportunity to offer me a bouquet of flowers. I am counting on you to alert me if you notice a gentleman who appears more lovestruck than most.

MAGGIE   Rest assured I'll let you know. Until then, we would be well advised to review your speech.

A knock at the door.

THE QUEEN   Come in. Perhaps that's him arriving early with his bouquet!

MR. CLARK enters.

MR. CLARK   Your Majesty, I have the latest news from the docks. As we hoped, Titanica's appointment has stabilized the situation.

THE QUEEN   Has the army devised a plan to keep those wretches in check during the ceremony?

MR. CLARK   It will be very easy to keep an eye on them. They're all well known to the police. As you requested, the media presence will be limited: only your personal photographer will be allowed on site. That way, if the squatters try to manifest their discontent, the population will know nothing of it. I was also instructed to ask for a copy of your speech.

MAGGIE   We were just about to revise it.

THE QUEEN   You and the lords shall learn of its content tomorrow along with the rest of the nation.

Mr. CLARK I beg your pardon?

The QUEEN I am perfectly capable of writing this speech on my own.

MAGGIE Your Majesty, we don't doubt in the least the finesse of your writing style.

Mr. CLARK Absolutely not. But it would be preferable—

The QUEEN I will finish writing this speech on my own.

Mr. CLARK As you wish. However, given the delicate situation, I can't insist enough on the importance of subtlety.

The QUEEN Have you ever seen your Queen be anything but subtle?

❧ XVI ❧

Near the Thames.

JIMMY Eddy! Eddy! *(EDWARD enters.)* I convinced them. The King Edward squatters are taking up arms during the inauguration.

EDWARD Precious child. What is your plan?

JIMMY Just before the soldiers arrive, I'll climb up the crane and hide on the container. The others will be dispersed in the crowd, with Molotov cocktails under their clothes...

EDWARD Are you sure they'll be able to hide the weapons?

JIMMY Black Jack knows some soldiers he thinks he can bribe. After the Queen's speech, when everyone's clapping, we'll strike.

EDWARD It will be a memorable day!

JIMMY I will be carrying the most dangerous, the most subversive weapon of all: a video camera. I'll film the squatters' rebellion from my vantage point on the container. Raw images that we can send around the world to fuel the fires of revolt!

EDWARD The hour of my revenge is finally at hand. After seven centuries in the shadows, I will settle the score with this country, with these men and women who exile the object of their fears. Precious child, your courage moves me.

JIMMY Back in America, I felt a huge cry of rage rising inside me. I couldn't sleep at night. I was on constant watch, my eyes glued to the computer screen. Wars, famines, genocides and acts of terrorism all formed one reality that filled me with a sense of revolt. Images from everywhere—from other centuries, from other countries—penetrated my psyche through the window of my eyes. I would get up, my temples pulsing, my fists raised, ready to join in the battle, to let out a great shout, a cry for revolution! But I always came back to my senses, back to the basement of our quiet house in the middle of the night, back to my sleepy suburb, peaceful as a cemetery. Tomorrow, the images I film will travel into living rooms and shake up all those who think the world is as comfortable as their sofa.

EDWARD And Piers Gaveston, the King Edward squatters, all those they want banished from this island will finally be avenged. Take this cloak, which for centuries has helped me blend into the crowd. It will keep you safe.

VOICE OF ISABELLA Edward, is that you? I recognize your voice!

EDWARD Oh, good heavens! It's her!

VOICE OF ISABELLA Edward!

EDWARD Do me a favour, young friend: stall her.

EDWARD leaves on the run.

৩ XVII ৲

*Queen ISABELLA enters holding a metallic muzzle that
she hides behind her back. JIMMY, clad in EDWARD's
cloak, has his back to her.*

ISABELLA   Edward, there you are. Perhaps we could bury the
hatchet tonight. We've been hounding each other for centuries
now, you refusing to forgive me, and both of us trapped
between heaven and earth in this vicious circle of unuttered
pardon. Surely you don't plan on holding a grudge until the
end of time? I'm asking for your forgiveness, Edward. The
sister of the King of France, your wife before God and man, is
asking for your forgiveness. *(A beat, then she slowly approaches
JIMMY.)* This is childish, Edward. We're making fools of
ourselves in front of all these strangers. You know very well
that I had nothing against your lover. It was my sovereign
duty to have him deported. Piers was a nice boy, a touch
frivolous... *(With extreme precaution, she gets ready to put the
muzzle on him, but at the last minute, JIMMY turns around. She is
momentarily stunned.)* Piers Gaveston! It wasn't enough that
you soiled our coat of arms, now you insist on coming back to
haunt us. And he gave you his cloak, you, his favourite, his
pet.

JIMMY   I'm not who you think I am.

ISABELLA   Had he remained king, he would have gone so far as
to have you crowned, you pervert! Well, two can play at this
game, knight of fallen morals! You may have his cape, but I
have his sword! *(She takes out a sword from under her skirt and
brandishes it.)* You alone are the black evil devouring the roots
of our island. You, who slithered into the arms of a sovereign,
making him leave wife, child and subjects to indulge in the
most vile of all passions, you won't get away this time, Piers
Gaveston!

JIMMY   *(removing his finery)* You are mistaken, ma'am.

ISABELLA   Who on earth are you? You have five seconds to give
me a straight answer or I'll pierce your heart.

JIMMY   An American activist come to do battle.

ISABELLA   Steer clear, young man, of battles that aren't yours to fight. You could end up dying disguised as someone else. Who gave you that cloak?

JIMMY   A beggar.

ISABELLA   A king, you liar! In the future, mind your own affairs. You won't escape me, Edward!

She exits.

ॐ XVIII ॐ

*Inauguration day. Drum roll. MAGGIE and MR.
CLARK at the foot of the platform. TITANICA enters,
accompanied by VIVIAN. MR. CLARK goes to meet
them.*

MR. CLARK   Madam, there you are. At last.

TITANICA   I exhausted myself getting ready. I needed a little
beauty rest.

MR. CLARK   William Clark, Her Majesty's official spokesperson.

TITANICA   You've hardly changed at all.

MR. CLARK   Thank you. You, too, seem timeless.

TITANICA   This is my lady in waiting, Miss Vivian.

MR. CLARK   *Enchanté.*

TITANICA   Vivian is preparing a documentary on me.

MR. CLARK   A young filmmaker, how charming!

VIVIAN   I'm actually an art historian. I don't claim to be—

TITANICA   Stop underestimating yourself, Vivian. Your work
is *très* avant-garde.

MAGGIE   *(to MR. CLARK)* A restoration is clearly in order.

THE QUEEN enters.

TITANICA   Your Majesty! You are radiant! That hairstyle will
go down in history, I'm sure. Was your drive here pleasant?

THE QUEEN   Indeed. Thank you, sir.

MR. CLARK   Madam, Your Majesty. One says madam to an artist's
muse.

TITANICA   You look absolutely delicious in that gown. May I kiss
your cheek?

THE QUEEN   *(insincere)* I like your gown, too…. It…

MR. CLARK It's got panache.

MAGGIE Your Majesty, perhaps it's time for a little touch-up.

> *MAGGIE hands THE QUEEN a small mirror and a
> tube of lipstick. THE QUEEN applies the lipstick.*

TITANICA What a fabulous red!

THE QUEEN Thank you.

TITANICA May I?

THE QUEEN *(revolted but polite)* Why not?

TITANICA *(applying the lipstick)* Oh, *quel rouge!* I haven't been this
frivolous in years! You know, at my age, it is a bit harsh. And
with the lighting on the docks, the effect can be ghastly. But
for an occasion like this…

> *Another drum roll.*

THE QUEEN The hour is at hand!

TITANICA Ah!

MAGGIE While the Queen is giving her speech to the journalists,
Mr. Clark will brief you on the details of your restoration.

TITANICA I…

MAGGIE You will meet with the media after Her Majesty has left.

THE QUEEN A squash tournament calls me elsewhere. It was a
pleasure meeting you, Ms. Titanica.

MR. CLARK Ladies and gentlemen: Her Majesty, The Queen of
England.

> *THE QUEEN appears on the platform, while TITANICA
> takes a seat off to the side with MR. CLARK, VIVIAN
> and MAGGIE.*

THE QUEEN *(reading)* Loyal and faithful subjects of England, on
this memorable day, your Queen appears before you, in love.
For if the law of blood dictates that you must obey me, it also
dictates that I, as your Queen, must obey, like a servile lover,

a force that reigns above me: duty. Duty is the only lover a sovereign must serve.... *Servile sovereigns? Servile, I am servile. Hanging on your every word, I am but foam and froth, like the agitated waters that churn with the passing of a ship... a ship.* The shimmer and grandeur of the arts may sometimes move and bewitch a sovereign, but it is ultimately to duty that royal hearts turn and return.... *To the earth, this earth with which God has entrusted me and to which, under your weight, my lover, I dream to be pinned. You, my lover, could teach me everything, from the fragility of hierarchies to the stunning regularity of the tides, teach me that anything can enter one's blood, that blackness can taint the blue, that love can release its bitter vinegar....* A sovereign's fate may seem bitter, but it is with humility that we accept this fate and when we offer our bodies, it is to duty, of which we are the puppets, mere instruments.... *Beware the spittle of a poet, ladies. Should it make its way up your thigh, alter its course with a firm hand. Protect your precious mound from its furious semen. Today, a queen's virtue is devastated; flames are lapping at the abyss....* O duty, my eternal lover, at your feet I lay my frail and mortal destiny. *I am nothing but fire, secretions and blood!*

> *Blood trickles down from the container and lands on* THE QUEEN's *head.*

Blood!

> *Bodies fall from the sky. Widespread panic.* JIMMY *is standing on the container, dressed in* EDWARD's *cloak, video camera in hand.*

❧ XIX ❧

The docks at night. The place is deserted. The moon shines down on the basin. A body is floating on the surface.

JIMMY   Eddy! Eddy! *(EDWARD enters.)* Something terrible has happened. I was standing on the container, scanning the crowd with my video camera, when the image suddenly blurred. Decomposing bodies started appearing through the lens… I thought I was dreaming, and then I realized. Corpses, hundreds of corpses were falling from the container, falling on the crowd gathered below. They weren't flowers, Eddy!

EDWARD   I know.

JIMMY   You knew?

EDWARD   Yes. From the very beginning.

JIMMY   And you didn't say anything!

EDWARD   I feared you might back out.

JIMMY   Are you the one who slashed the container?

EDWARD   I had to reveal this terrible plot to the nation.

JIMMY   Who are they, Eddy?

EDWARD   They are the flowers that fair England would rather see grow in fields far from her own. Young men and women, children and the elderly, drug addicts, outcasts, haemophiliacs and ordinary citizens who lost their lives to tainted blood and whose bodies have yet to be claimed.

JIMMY   But what about these gardens everyone's talking about?

EDWARD   A clandestine cemetery where saintly England planned to bury them. But now, the Crown will not come out of this unscathed. Thanks to you, Jimmy, my vengeance is now complete.

JIMMY   You may have avenged your deported lover, but you've awakened a thousand other desires for vengeance. Opened a thousand other wounds. The worst of all happened after, Eddy. The soldiers cleaned everything up, leaving the docks deserted and immaculate. It was as though nothing had happened. Until a forgotten corpse that had sunk deep into the waters of the basin floated to the surface and the moon lit his face...

ISADORA enters screaming and hiding her face in her hands.

⤳ XX ⤶

> BLACK JACK, TITANICA, VIVIAN, JIMMY and the
> band of squatters run to the edge of the basin and
> surround ISADORA.

ISADORA Close his eyes, I implore you! Close his eyes!

VIVIAN Who are you talking about, Isadora? Who is she talking about?

ISADORA I'm talking about him, floating like a lily pad on the water, staring at the sky with his eyes wide open, gazing at the moon like an abandoned child. I can't bear to look at him. Close his eyes. He is my brother.

> A beat, then everyone approaches the basin, troubled.
> ISADORA stays back.

BLACK JACK It's him all right.

ISADORA Please, someone, close his eyes. Go down into the basin and close his eyes.

> A beat, then JIMMY takes off his shoes, rolls up his pant
> legs and goes toward the water.

TITANICA No. You must do it, Isadora.

ISADORA I can't. Not without my veil.

TITANICA It is your duty. You are his sister.

ISADORA No! I refuse for him to see my hideous face.

TITANICA He already knows your face. It's but a reflection of his own pain. You owe it to him.

> A beat, then ISADORA removes her hands from her face
> and slowly approaches her brother's body.

ISADORA My brother I never knew, my brave, beloved brother, do not fear the woman coming toward you. She's neither beautiful nor crowned, but she loves you and wishes you no harm. Forgive me for not protecting you from our mother's madness that shattered me. What does destiny have in store for you? (*She closes his eyes.*) Don't you find it darker all of a sudden?

TITANICA   We must take him out of the water, Isadora. Bury him in the earth.

ISADORA   No! No one's touching him. I will watch over him tonight, here, in these waters. I will wrap him up in the Union Jack to keep him from the cold and in the morning, I will lead him in a hero's march to his final resting place. I will avenge you, Lewis. No one is touching him. He is my brother. I am his sister.

ISADORA exits.

TITANICA   Forgive me, my children. I must have been living somewhere else. In the past, just like you've always said, Black Jack. I thought I could help you. I thought my meeting with the Queen would save us all, but the day draws to a close in blood and tears. I have been naive. I believed the world to be less damaged than it really is.

TITANICA exits.

∽ XXI ∾

The royal quarters. MAGGIE and MR. CLARK.

MAGGIE The celestial ballet has ended, the sky is overcast, a storm is gathering. Those images filmed by that young boy, that stranger who appeared on the container out of God knows where, dressed like a vision from the past—those images made their way around the entire kingdom within a matter of hours.

MR. CLARK Rumour has it he's a foreigner, an illegal alien from America. It's still possible to make him disappear.

MAGGIE I'm afraid it's too late for that. That young man has become the poster boy for all of England, the inspiration for an aborted revolution and the chief witness to one of the biggest political scandals of all time. The journalists will find him, he'll tell his story, and a thousand years of royal obedience—the principles of an entire civilization—will come crashing down, all because of a few cadavers piled up in a container that an adolescent opened by mistake.

MR. CLARK For security reasons, I have ordered that all the possessions of the young woman who was with Titanica be seized and that any video equipment be destroyed. We should have reinforced security. This is all my fault.

MAGGIE Stop whipping yourself. We are all to blame. The Queen and her anonymous lover, you and your Titanica…

MR. CLARK How is the Queen?

MAGGIE She has locked herself in her quarters and keeps saying that young man is the reincarnation of a past demon.

MR. CLARK How could we not have foreseen this threat to the kingdom? Where did we go wrong?

MAGGIE The purity of blood: that is what we should have preserved in this country, the purity of blood. But we must now face the music, Mr. Clark. It is but a question of hours before the kingdom is overthrown.

∽ XXII ∾

The docks. The same night. BLACK JACK is alone on stage, dressed in a soldier's uniform with a bottle in his hand. JIMMY enters.

JIMMY I come on Isadora's behalf. Tomorrow at dawn, a procession will leave from the docks to carry DJ Lewis's body to the city square. The more of us there are, the more difficult it will be for them to deny this monstrous story…

BLACK JACK By that time, I might already be far from here, far out at sea, far far south…

JIMMY You've been drinking, Black Jack. Let me talk.

BLACK JACK Yes, I've been drinking. But not enough to erase all those bodies from my mind. What are they exiling? The pain of living we all share? Then send me too! From the moment we're born, life makes us feel as though we're nothing. And yet we insist like obstinate lovers who refuse to acknowledge the polite signs of rejection. Has life ever made you feel loved, Jimmy?

JIMMY You've got no right to tell me life has no place for me! I crossed the Atlantic to find a meaning for mine!

BLACK JACK You could have stayed where you were.

JIMMY I'll make a place for myself, whether life likes it or not… is that clear?

BLACK JACK Come and see what life has in store for you, Jimmy!

> *BLACK JACK forces JIMMY into the basin beside DJ Lewis's floating body.*

Do you think life made him feel loved? Imagine his flesh being eaten away by the disease, his cry of agony when he was pinned to his hospital bed and the insatiable, invisible beast gnawed away at his skin and bones! *(A beat, then JIMMY starts crying. BLACK JACK takes JIMMY in his arms and becomes very gentle.)* And now look how the water is rocking him tonight, how the light of the moon is gently caressing him…

so gently, you could almost imagine there are no marks on his body, no suffering in his bones. Has anyone ever rocked you like death is rocking him tonight? Has a word ever brought you the solace the moon is giving him tonight? *(He moves away from JIMMY.)* Not me. That's why I'm putting my uniform back on and joining the troops on the side of death.

JIMMY   What are you talking about?

BLACK JACK   The army will grant me a pardon. When I tell them what I saw, they'll want to buy my silence. They'll reinstate me. I was a corporal.

> *BLACK JACK puts on his hat, the final touch to make his uniform complete.*

JIMMY   You're just asking for trouble. They'll get rid of you!

BLACK JACK   I've found my cause. Isn't that what we're all looking for? A cause to hide behind, to make us feel like we really exist. A word to the wise, kid: jump on the first boat heading home, leave, save your skin, before the army gets its hands on you.

> *BLACK JACK exits.*

❧ XXIII ❧

*Stormy night. The royal quarters. THE QUEEN, alone,
leafing through a history book.*

THE QUEEN   Where is he? There must be a picture of that angel-
faced devil somewhere! *(She stops on a page.)* There you are,
knight of vice! So I was right.... Piers Gaveston has returned
to London to avenge himself, to splatter me—ME—with the
blood of perverts! *(In the shadows, a figure appears.)* Who's
there? Who dares to enter my most private refuge? O, lover of
the docks and the underground, have you come to release me,
to carry me away on horseback, far from all this?

Queen ISABELLA enters.

ISABELLA   Don't get too excited, *ma chère*. It's just me.

THE QUEEN   Isabella, the She-Wolf of France.... Is this the night
when the dead rise from their graves to strike fear in the
hearts of the living?

ISABELLA   We escaped the yellowing pages of our history books
long ago.

THE QUEEN   My distant ancestor, to what do I owe the honour?

ISABELLA   I know who struck your ship earlier this week and
who did the very same this morning with a container full of
corpses.

THE QUEEN   Piers Gaveston!

ISABELLA   No. That young man is but a pale copy fresh from
America that Edward flattered into submission. The real
culprit is Edward, Edward who, for seven centuries, has
never forgiven me for deporting his favourite.

THE QUEEN   So Edward II is as stubborn as legend would have it.
You did a brave, admirable thing coming between him and
his lover.

ISABELLA That Piers was the devil incarnate. He jeopardized the traditions of our monarchy. Piers Gaveston had to be deported.

THE QUEEN Like all those corpses eaten away by their own vice and with whom contact could corrupt both body and soul. Their contaminated blood even trickled down my breast!

ISABELLA I know how to put an end to the curse and stop Edward from biting.

THE QUEEN How?

ISABELLA I'll need some strapping soldiers.

THE QUEEN Do you think a few men will be enough to satisfy his appetite?

ISABELLA Satisfy his appetite, no. But put this muzzle on him, this muzzle that an artist—or rather his assistant—was kind enough to make, yes.

THE QUEEN Alas, you overestimate our soldiers. They couldn't even dispose of a few miserable wretches!

ISABELLA Edward isn't as invincible as you might think. We have bait. Don't forget his soft spot: his passion for that no-good Gaveston. Or for someone who bears a disturbing resemblance to the young knight...

THE QUEEN Cunning Isabella.

ISABELLA Supply me with the men, and I'll do the rest. Oh, yes, I almost forgot... *(She takes an envelope out of her corset.)* I found this on your balcony! Good night, Your Majesty.

ISABELLA exits.

THE QUEEN A new letter! Thank God he's still alive! *(reading)* "Virginia, if only our bodies, our saliva and our blood could mix to form a bond from which would come a man, a man who would be neither king nor beggar, a man freed from your chains of monarchy and from my chains of destitution, a man who would simply be human and whose eyes would reflect not the bloody memories of past eras, but rather that elusive and luminous thing called the future. But perhaps my love arrives too late in the string of eras so neatly catalogued in our history books. Sad from so much hoping, I attempt one last meeting. I'll be waiting for you tonight on the King Edward dock." Me, on the docks, at night! As a woman and not as a queen? Maggie!

MAGGIE enters.

Prepare my travel attire, we're going down to the gutter.

∾ XXIV ∾

At TITANICA's. VIVIAN and JIMMY are at her side.

TITANICA   You're quiet today, my children.

VIVIAN   I don't know how to tell you this, Titanica. The army stormed Asher's place; the soldiers destroyed all of my reels. Nothing is left of our interviews.

A beat.

TITANICA   Silence and oblivion have been nipping at my heels for some time now. Spurred on by your patience and kindness, I tried one last time to fight them off. We should have known it was a losing battle.

VIVIAN   We'll find a solution. We'll start from the beginning, with a little patience and courage. Don't underestimate your importance, or that of the greater family to which you belong: Art.

TITANICA   Art... such pretension, such an illusion! Art is lovely, Art dazzles us, but Art, my children, cannot change the world or its deadly course. Me, Titanica, the Great Battle Gown? I've been nothing but a tiny, insignificant heap of metal in this long procession of blood, tears, victories and defeats that we still insist on calling Humanity.

VIVIAN   That's not true.

TITANICA   It is true. The proof is that in 1968, I stood for a new era in this country, a great liberation. Everything was supposed to change. But tonight, I don't want to be called to do battle. I want to reclaim my freedom, live the life that thirty years of art stole from me.

JIMMY   But isn't now your moment of truth? You could walk with us at the head of the procession. Tomorrow at dawn, Isadora will avenge her brother and all the others they want deported.

TITANICA   What use would this suit of armour be to all those poor dead people? This armour was supposed to protect me;

instead it imprisoned me, destroyed me and ended up
making a victim of me. The Victim's Gown, that's what
Edmund should have called me.

JIMMY   So you're not coming?

TITANICA   I'm too old and too weak to fight such a battle.

VIVIAN   It's as though you've lost your faith in art...

TITANICA   In the face of all the madness in the world, art is a
small speck, full of good intentions, but futile all the same.

VIVIAN   You don't believe a word you're saying! Haven't you
devoted your entire life to art?

TITANICA   Yes. My life, my youth. And I'm not saying that those
who do the same after me are wrong. Sometimes it's worth
the sacrifice, even for a lost cause. All I know is that it was the
wrong choice for me.... It was.... How shall I put it? Too
heavy. I'm sure that you, Vivian, can understand that.

VIVIAN   Yes. Of course.

TITANICA   Now, go get ready for this procession.... Off you go!

> *VIVIAN and JIMMY start to leave. Then JIMMY turns
> around.*

JIMMY   You are dishonest and pathetic.

VIVIAN   Jimmy!

JIMMY   What kind of coward is hiding under that gown?

VIVIAN   Jimmy, you don't know what you're saying!

JIMMY   I don't care. What kind of coward abandons a cause he
chose to defend? You are a coward. You disguised your true
self. You didn't accept this cause out of courage; you did it to
shield your weakness and your fear of living.

TITANICA   Yes, I was afraid, Jimmy. Fear—

JIMMY   I have no respect for you.

VIVIAN   Jimmy!

JIMMY   Do you even remember the boy you were at twenty?

TITANICA   Come here, Jimmy! Look at me.

JIMMY   You disgust me.

TITANICA   Look at me.

>   *A beat, then JIMMY finally looks TITANICA in the eye.*

I was just like you.

>   *JIMMY exits.*

❧ XXV ❧

The docks. It is night. THE QUEEN enters, followed by her reader, who pushes her forward.

The QUEEN This place is too dark and too cold to harbour a man of such luminous poetry!

MAGGIE I know nothing of poetry, but I do know how to read a map. Go on!

The QUEEN Don't rush me! I must be very careful where I step. Imagine the horror if he were sleeping on the ground and the heel of my shoe were to pierce his heart…

MAGGIE Well, that would just be Cupid finishing off what he started.

BLACK JACK appears from the shadows and stands tall in front of them.

The QUEEN Oh, a soldier. Perhaps you could help us, brave guardian of order.

BLACK JACK You little ladies looking for something? A man, perhaps?

The QUEEN Yes—

MAGGIE No! We were just going for a walk.

BLACK JACK A walk on the docks… to breathe in some fresh ocean air, no doubt?

MAGGIE Yes. Madam suffers from respiratory troubles.

BLACK JACK Ah! And you think you can walk around here, just like that, without answering to anyone?

MAGGIE We aren't doing anything wrong. We are two respectable women—

BLACK JACK This is private property. You're trespassing.

The QUEEN This is my kingdom. These docks are the property of the state.

BLACK JACK What?

MAGGIE What madam meant to say is that we are all masters of our own kingdom. Could you tell us who reigns over these docks so we can apologize?

BLACK JACK takes a knife out of his pocket.

BLACK JACK Here, the master is the one with the longest knife.

THE QUEEN Oh!

MAGGIE I see... well then, our sincere apologies... Mr.?

BLACK JACK Knife.

MAGGIE Good night, Mr. Knife.

They start to leave.

BLACK JACK Oy!

MAGGIE Yes?

BLACK JACK The toll?

MAGGIE Oh, of course.... How much?

BLACK JACK *(snatching her purse)* That ought to do.

MAGGIE Splendid...

BLACK JACK Have a nice walk, ladies.

MAGGIE Thank you.

BLACK JACK exits.

THE QUEEN My God, Maggie, call a taxi, let's go home this instant! This is a hostile world, these people are predators. Even the soldiers are corrupt. Nothing here has the sweetness of my lover's words. Nothing, I tell you!

MAGGIE Finally, a sensible decision, Your Majesty.

They are about to leave, when THE QUEEN stops suddenly in her tracks, struck by a familiar sound.

ISADORA Sleep, my brother Lewis, sleep. I will watch over you, the only lantern in this starless night. Sleep, Lewis…

The QUEEN Ah! Do you hear that, Maggie? A voice, poetry…

> *In the shadows, not far from THE QUEEN and her reader, we see ISADORA, on the edge of the basin, keeping watch over her dead brother.*

That language, that rhythm… it's reminiscent of his.

MAGGIE But it's a woman, Your Majesty.

The QUEEN Listen!

ISADORA Sleep, my brother, to the angels I entrust your flight.

The QUEEN A poetess. No doubt from the same literary circle. Come.

MAGGIE I think it would be preferable—

The QUEEN I must speak to her. We won't have risked our lives in vain.

MAGGIE Be careful, Your Majesty, we don't know these people.

The QUEEN Miss! Miss!

> *ISADORA sees THE QUEEN and is momentarily stunned. THE QUEEN, for her part, has trouble hiding how disturbed she is by ISADORA's face.*

ISADORA You came.

The QUEEN We are looking for a poet who signs his poems "The lover of the docks and the underground." We came on foot from the city to say hello. Could you lead us to him?

ISADORA Of course. But we must be quiet. His sleep is very fragile.

> *ISADORA, THE QUEEN and MAGGIE go towards the basin.*

An angel, a speck of galactic dust put on this earth to bear the weight of the world…

THE QUEEN Miss, this poet is as dear to me as a son. And if it weren't for laws and propriety, I would have him crowned at dawn.

MAGGIE Your Majesty!

THE QUEEN Duty and royalty have their imperatives, but so too does love.

ISADORA Take my hand, and come into the water where Lewis is resting. Lewis, thanks to whom our hearts finally beat to the same rhythm.

> *ISADORA, THE QUEEN and MAGGIE go into the basin and make their way towards DJ Lewis's floating body. Faced with his rotting corpse, THE QUEEN and MAGGIE are momentarily speechless, horrified.*

Lewis, Her Majesty the Queen of England has come to pay her respects…

THE QUEEN This man has been dead for days! He cannot be the one who just this morning wrote me a passionate letter. Such fire, such life, such ardour couldn't possibly come from the dead!

> *A beat.*

ISADORA "My Queen, my pussy, my beacon, my lady…" "If only our bodies, our saliva and our blood could mix…" "Virginia, my mouth on your skin…" I read them all. All his rough drafts. To get a better sense of who he was. And I brought you the last letter, the one he left unfinished on his deathbed.

> *A beat, then THE QUEEN takes out the letter and looks at it.*

What was he looking for? We'll never know. But his words brought you down here tonight. Ask him for forgiveness. It won't change a thing. But do it anyway.

THE QUEEN Let go of my hand, Miss.

ISADORA Remember that only moments ago, you arrived, your heart full of love…

The QUEEN   Here in this place, I see nothing worthy of being called love. Remove this horror from my sight!

MAGGIE   Come, Your Majesty, let's return to the palace.

THE QUEEN and MAGGIE exit.

ᨠ XXVI ᨢ

*The docks. ISADORA is preparing her brother's body.
The squatters come out of the shadows and stand around
her.*

ISADORA I will carry you, my brother. I swear: neither the tides
nor the sailors will carry you to your final resting place. In all
of London, I will walk, demanding a show of respect. People
will cry out: "Who is that disfigured woman embracing a
rotting corpse?" But I will continue, my head held high,
shouting to the onlookers that your destroyed flesh that
dirties my hands is the only thing I've loved in all my life. In
our wake, all the wretches who recognize us as their own will
follow, and a true march of the downtrodden will accompany
us to the place where our mother always dreamed we would
end up: Buckingham Palace. We'll enter the hall under the
bewildered gaze of the guards. We'll climb the stairs, leaving
everyone speechless, our misery imposing its reign. Right up
to the Queen's immaculate bed. All of England will learn that
we, with our blood links to the gutters, are resting where, by
virtue of our noble hearts, we should have been born. It is for
you, my brother, that today the world order will be
overturned. For you, and for you alone, DJ Lewis.

The procession begins. TITANICA stays back, alone.

TITANICA O black night that follows the bright day when heaven
returned to the living their most shameful dead... What will
your final fury unleash? Promise me that tomorrow the world
will be different. Now, where might I find a tool shed?

❧ XXVII ❧

The royal quarters. The Queen *and her reader.*

Maggie Your Majesty, a strange noise is coming from the streets. From the window, I saw a crowd, a procession that seems to be marching straight on the palace. It's as though I can feel the presence of that woman, Isadora, at the head of the swarm of flies. Vengeance… she is outraged and seeking vengeance!

The Queen Anything else, Maggie?

Maggie I'm afraid. Flies, Your Majesty, feed on rotting flesh. I have a terrible premonition: blood and pillage, iron bars and sharp teeth.

The Queen Anything else, Maggie?

Maggie Death is at our door. You must do something. I don't know, set the dogs on them, they haven't eaten for a week. An order, Your Majesty, a single order. Do something! An order and I swear, I'll obey!

The Queen An order. A single order? Get my botany book and read our national poet's magnificent inscription. It will be a welcome change from the corrupt verses of the underground.

A beat, MAGGIE, trembling, begins to read.

Maggie (*reading*)
"O lush England, from the skies where I admire you
I exclaim before your scarlet red meadows
Unfolding like smooth and silky velvet
Planted like an insult under a steely grey sky
O lush England, where does your misery hide?
Your splendour astounds me
You upon whom the sun so rarely shines
The sun so rarely shines"

Sound of windows being broken.

THE QUEEN I know, Maggie, that you aren't a fan of poetry. But the red stains of which the poet speaks, how do you see them? Like poppies or like bloodstains?

> MR. CLARK enters.

MR. CLARK They are asking to see you, Your Majesty.

THE QUEEN Let them in.

❧ XXVIII ❧

*The same night. Through the fog, we see JIMMY dressed
as a medieval knight, gagged and tied to a rock
overlooking the Thames. EDWARD enters and sees him
from behind.*

EDWARD My God! Could it be? Mist, if this cruel vision is your
handiwork, dissipate this instant! *(He waits.)* Piers....
My love, finally avenged, you have returned! *(EDWARD
comes a bit closer.)* The hair, the delicate body, the proud air,
that way you have of never bending in the wind. Your body
so fine, so fragile, and yet so solid when standing before
nature's fury. You're still looking out to the sea, my love!
(Gagged, JIMMY lets out a few sounds.) What say you, my pet?
Are you telling the tide to stop its clamouring? Only you are
mad enough to try. I knew that one day the tide, in its infinite
generosity, would bring you back to me. *(EDWARD comes
closer to JIMMY. He is about to put his hand on JIMMY's shoulder
but hesitates.)* Forces of heaven and earth, keep this beautiful
vision from evaporating at the touch of my hand. Dearest
love, if my touch casts you back to the realm of memory, I
want to tell you one last time, before reaching out to you,
that I loved you more than my country. *(EDWARD touches
JIMMY's shoulder with the tips of his fingers.)* Piers!

> *EDWARD embraces JIMMY. At the same time,
> ISABELLA and three soldiers appear and grab
> EDWARD. They exit with him, leaving JIMMY alone.*

❧ XXIX ❧

JIMMY, still tied to the rock. VIVIAN enters, suitcase in hand.

VIVIAN *(removing the gag)* Jimmy, what happened? Who did this to you?

JIMMY Untie me, Vivian! They took Eddy. Hurry. They want to stop him from biting. Eddy!

VIVIAN hurries to untie him.

VIVIAN You're tired, Jimmy. You're delirious. You need to rest.

JIMMY No! We need to do something for Eddy. Let's find Titanica. I'll apologize and she'll help us. *(calling)* Titanica!

VIVIAN It's no use, Jimmy. There's no one here.

They search the whole dock. They end up finding TITANICA's gown, opened and abandoned in a corner, a blowtorch at its side.

She who so wanted to go for a swim. Maybe once freed she felt so light that she flew away. Or maybe her bones crumbled after being released from their brace…

JIMMY She left before I had a chance to apologize.

A beat, then JIMMY approaches the gown and kneels down. He looks inside and turns to face VIVIAN.

VIVIAN The line? What is it?

JIMMY *(reading)* "Fight other people's battles and you wage war; fight your own and you live your life." *(a beat)* Vivian, what battle can I fight? What story will I be the hero of? Or will I be remembered as nothing more than the witness of horror?

VIVIAN By marching on the palace, Isadora and her procession are ending a battle. You still have your life ahead of you. That's a lot. I'm leaving, too. I've catalogued all of Asher's work. Goodbye, Jimmy.

She kisses him and goes to leave.

JIMMY   *(handing her the camera)* Vivian! I found your camera.

VIVIAN   I don't need it anymore. Keep it. Maybe it's your turn to immortalize something.

She exits.

❧ XXX ❧

JIMMY, alone on stage. He starts recording himself.

JIMMY   I don't know who I'm talking to, but I have a question for you. Do my eyes reflect anything other than the bloody memory of centuries gone by? Anything other than fear? I'm afraid. Afraid of dying before giving anything back. Afraid of losing my lustre before I've ever shone. Afraid of being carried away to the flowering land of exile. I wish I'd been born with a mission that a gypsy could read in the palm of my hand. Born with a cross to bear. I'm afraid of returning home without finding anything here, without following in the steps of a hero. Of returning alone on the seas, in search of something I alone must find. The only battle that is mine: my life in the current of yours.

Curtain.

SÉBASTIEN HARRISSON

photo by: David Harrison

A graduate of the playwriting program of the National Theatre School of Canada, Sébastien Harrisson is one of the most unique and innovative voices among young Quebec playwrights. *Floes* and *Titanica* have been produced in both Quebec and France. He has also written plays for young audiences, including *Stanlislas Walter LeGrand* and *D'Alaska*, which have toured all around Quebec. Sébastien was a finalist for the Governor General's Literary Award for *Floes* and *D'Alaska (suite nordique)*. His work has been translated into English, Flemish, Spanish and German.

CRYSTAL BELIVEAU

photo by: Renaud Séguin

Crystal is a writer and translator. Her creative non-fiction has appeared in *Prairie Fire* and *Liberté*. In addition to *Titanica*, she has translated *Le Long de la Principale* (*Down the Main Drag*) by Steve Laplante, which received a Betty nomination for Best Original Play in 2004. She is currently at work on the English translation of *Portrait chinois d'une imposteure* (*Chinese Portrait of an Impostor*) by Dominick Parenteau-Lebeuf, slated to appear in the third volume of *Anthology of Québec Women's Plays in English Translation*.